# Moving Day

**Written by Jo S. Kittinger**

**Illustrated by Ilene Richard**

Children's Press®
A Division of Scholastic Inc.
New York • Toronto • London • Auckland • Sydney
Mexico City • New Delhi • Hong Kong
Danbury, Connecticut

**For Joan Broerman, who started me writing and kept me writing**
—J.S.K.

**To my wonderful family**
—I.R.

Reading Consultants

**Linda Cornwell**
Literacy Specialist

**Katharine A. Kane**
Education Consultant
(Retired, San Diego County Office of Education
and San Diego State University)

Library of Congress Cataloging-in-Publication Data

Kittinger, Jo S.
   Moving day / written by Jo S. Kittinger ; illustrated by Ilene
Richard.
      p. cm. — (Rookie reader)
Summary: After a girl says good-bye to friends, she and her family load
up the car and head for their new house.
   ISBN 0-516-22846-3 (lib. bdg.)        0-516-27784-7 (pbk.)
   [1. Moving, Household—Fiction. 2. Stories in rhyme.]  I. Richard, Ilene, ill.
II. Title. III. Series.
   PZ8.3.K65637 Mo 2003
   [E]—dc21
                                    2002008785

CHILDREN'S PRESS, AND A ROOKIE READER®, and associated logos are trademarks
and or registered trademarks of Grolier Publishing Co., Inc. SCHOLASTIC and associated
logos are trademarks and or registered trademarks of Scholastic Inc.
1 2 3 4 5 6 7 8 9 10 R 12 11 10 09 08 07 06 05 04 03

Pack my clothes.

3

Pack my toys.

Say good-bye to the girls and boys.

Load the truck.
Load the car.

Our new home is very far.

11

Stop for gas.
Stop for dinner.

13

Play a game.
I'm the winner!

Here's our town.

Here's our street.
Are there any kids to meet?

19

Here's our house.
There's so much space.

21

I think I'm going to like this place!

# Word List (50 words)

| | | | | |
|---|---|---|---|---|
| a | for | I'm | our | there |
| and | game | is | pack | there's |
| any | gas | kids | place | think |
| are | girls | like | play | this |
| boys | going | load | say | to |
| car | good-bye | meet | so | town |
| clothes | here's | moving | space | toys |
| day | home | much | stop | truck |
| dinner | house | my | street | very |
| far | I | new | the | winner |

## About the Author

Jo S. Kittinger, a native of Florida, lived in several states before settling in Alabama. A love of books and a passion to create inspires Jo to write both fiction and nonfiction books for children. Jo enjoys pottery, photography, and reading in her spare time. While teaching her own children to read, Jo realized the critical role of emergent readers. She wrote this book while moving her son, Robert, into college.

## About the Illustrator

Ilene Richard was a successful jewelry designer before getting back to illustrating children's books. She has illustrated many books in both the trade and educational markets. Ilene lives with her husband Lawrence, her daughter Jodi, her son Corey, and their dog Bess in Andover, Massachusetts.